Chasing the Dawn

40 devotional readings on pushing back the darkness

Catherine Campbell

MONARCH
BOOKS

Oxford, UK, and Grand Rapids, USA

Published by Monarch Books
an imprint of
Lion Hudson plc
Wilkinson House, Jordan Hill Road,
Oxford OX2 8DR, England
Email: monarch@lionhudson.com
www.lionhudson.com/monarch

ISBN 978 0 85721 738 7

First edition 2016

Acknowledgments
Unless otherwise stated scripture quotations taken from The Holy Bible, New King James Version © 1982 by Thomas Nelson, Inc. Used by permission. All right reserved. Scripture quotations marked NLT taken from the New Living Translation © 1996, 2004, 2007 by Tyndale House Foundation. Used by permission of Tyndale House Publishers, Inc., Carol Stream, Illinois 60188. Scripture quotations marked NIV taken from New International Version Anglicised © 1979, 1984, 2011 Biblica, formerly International Bible Society. Used by permission of Hodder & Stoughton Ltd, an Hachette UK company. All rights reserved. "NIV" is a registered trademark of Biblica. UK trademark number 1448790.

"Laid on Him" was written by Lance Pibworth, co-founder of UBM, and printed in YL Choruses 1997. Used with permission.

A catalogue record for this book is available from the British Library

Printed and bound in Malaysia, June 2016, LH01

Dedicated to
my granddaughter
Bethany,
for whom I would
chase any dawn.

"If I rise on the wings of the dawn,
if I settle on the far side of the sea,
even there your hand will guide me,
your right hand will hold me fast.
If I say, Surely the darkness will hide me
and the light become night around me,
even the darkness will not be dark to you;
the night will shine like the day,
for darkness is as light to you."

Psalm 139: 9–12 (NIV)

Foreword

It was a clear morning as I travelled along the road from Oxford to Burford when I had an epiphany. It was a simple and profound moment of realization that I think changed my understanding of the world for the better. I haven't been the same since. In my opinion that road is one of the most beautiful in England. As you head west towards Burford you drive along the side of a beautiful, verdant valley. The road sits on the top of one of the long sides of the valley and the landscape falls away to your right. If you catch it at the right time of day, the sun rises as you drive along the road and you feel as if you are watching a scene from a Turner painting. Powerful, simple, beautiful. That is exactly what happened to me on this particular morning.

As I drove along the road in the early morning darkness, my head was full of all that lay ahead. I was on my way to lecture at Regent's Theological College in Malvern and was running through the order of the day in my head. It was going to be a full and busy day. As I looked out the window, I saw the sun's rays begin to illuminate the landscape. The hitherto dark scene was being painted into animated life by the paintbrush of God and I was gobsmacked. I stopped the car to have a few moments peace and quiet and to enjoy this gift of stillness. Flask in hand I sipped hot coffee and stood silently as I contemplated my place in the world, the God that I served and the reality that He is with me always. Then it hit me.

The sun was not rising at all. How could it? The sun never rises. It moves and spins and shoots out solar flares and is engaged in a hundred other remarkable manoeuvres, but it doesn't rise. The sun never revolves around us. It doesn't rise or set. We move around the sun, it does not move around us. That simple reality had new weight on that beautiful morning.

I realised that the language I used often reflected the same kind of misunderstanding about God and me. God does not revolve around me. I revolve around him. I am not the centre of his universe, he is supposed to be the centre of mine. He does not chase after my every whim and fancy, I am called to live for his purposes and his glory.

That particular dawn changed my life. I hope and pray that as you read Catherine's brief reflections, you will experience a similar transformation.

Catherine's words are an open invitation to intimacy. They are crafted by a wordsmith whose choice of language is captivating, whose life is pregnant with the reality of God's strengthening and transforming presence and whose experience paints a rainbow across the sky of anyone who feels that God is always far away and therefore life is grey. Don't be fooled by the simplicity of her style. She draws you into the words of Scripture and their meaning with a power and intensity that is remarkable.

I will return to these words many times in the years that lie ahead. Each time I do so, I will remind myself that the dawn is certain every 24 hours. No darkness lasts forever. The night passes and the day springs into glorious life as a reminder to us that God is with us and we are never, ever alone.

When you rush through life you will miss the scenery around you but even more importantly, you run a high risk of missing where you are going and why. Far too many of us hurtle through our lives without a sense of purpose or direction. Let *Chasing the Dawn* become a pause button in your life. Use this little book to reconnect with God, his purpose for you and his promises to you. Let it remind you that the light is brighter than the darkness, always.

Malcolm Duncan
October 2015

Preface

I have come to love chasing the dawn.

Every Thursday morning for three years, I dragged my weary body behind the steering wheel of my little C3 and pointed it in a south-easterly direction. Early starts in spring and summer weren't too bad; it was the winter months that heightened my desire to hide under the duvet for just a few more minutes. But each week I resisted the urge and made it into the car while Coleraine remained cloaked in darkness. Barely a mile down the road I'd catch my first glimpse of the fine, thread-like grey line rising above the distant horizon. That first sight of weakness in the dark sky drew me on as I followed the procession of commuting vehicles leaving the north coast behind. Before long the headlights would bow to dawn's determination to supersede them, as muted yellows tinted the band of light deepening right before my eyes.

As the miles rolled past, familiar landmarks no longer hid behind the shadows of the night, every turn in the road now the visible evidence of a journey progressing. Near my journey's end anticipation eventually peaked as the light pushing back the darkness finally overwhelmed the sky. It's something that occurs every single day, yet watching it happen before your eyes always brings a smile. Darkness cannot stay where light shines.

In spite of the tiredness of the early start, I was never disappointed when I arrived at my destination. The excited sound of my granddaughter's voice from behind the front door made chasing the dawn more than worthwhile.

"Daddy, daddy!" she would shout. "Come quick! Granny Catherine's here!"

In Isaiah 9:2, 6 we read, "The people who walked in darkness have seen a great light; [...] For unto us a Child is born, unto us a Son is given; and the government will be upon His shoulder. And His name will be called Wonderful, Counselor, Mighty God, Everlasting Father, Prince of Peace."

Frequently I have had to "chase the dawn" in my own personal life, deep in my soul. During times when I thought the darkness of pain and grief was impossible to shift, I reached for the One described in Isaiah 9 as that "great light". With my eyes set on the journey ahead, He made it possible for the tiniest rift in the dark skies to produce the fine grey line that drew me on.

Then, as the light of His Word and the sun of His promises became brighter, the darkness had no other option but to give way, revealing once more the familiar signs of His comfort and peace.

I haven't reached my final destination yet, but I am already excited about the welcome I will receive from the One who continues faithfully to push back the darkness each and every day.

Of one thing I'm certain: "chasing the dawn" is definitely worth it!

Catherine Campbell

1

"Show me where I should walk, O Lord; point out the right road for me to follow. Lead me by your truth and teach me, for you are the God who saves me. All day long I put my hope in you."

Psalm 25: 4–5 (NLT)

It had been a beautiful evening when I had left home. In spite of the distance I had to travel, I had comforted myself with the thought that at least I would reach the event in daylight. One of spring's delights.

Returning to the car some hours later I discovered that more than darkness had fallen while the meeting was in progress. Even in the well-lit car park, mist hung like a woolly muffler around the lamp-globes, stealing the enjoyment of an evening that had gone well.

Fog! My worst driving nightmare.

As I left behind the streetlights on the town's boundary, I knew I was in for trouble. This was no annoying patch of local mist. Dense fog was obliterating even what should have been the most helpful markings for my journey home, the white line along the side of the road! I was driving – no, crawling – through what seemed like a solid block of murky grey, except for the fact that it allowed me to pass through it, as if by magic.

Just about convinced that I was on the correct side of the road, I inched the car forward, frightened that I was going to have to stop and abandon my journey. The thought terrified me. Would an oncoming vehicle be able to make out my parked car covered by this dangerous cloak? By now the steering wheel was wet with perspiration; I was confused and afraid, unable to make out where I was. Lost on a road I thought I knew.

"Lord!" I cried. "Please help me! I need a taillight to follow. Something to help guide me through this!"

The prayer had barely left my lips when a monster of a vehicle pulled out in front of me from a side road, totally oblivious to my presence on the road. I squealed with delight, for not only did the big truck have bold, bright rear fog lights, but also the expanse of both back doors was trimmed with an unbroken row of red lights! It might as well have spelled out "Follow Me!"

I've never been so excited about being stuck behind a lorry before.

And for the next fifteen miles I had my own personal guide through something I couldn't have managed on my own.

When David wrote Psalm 25 he was in his own personal fog. He still had enemies, had experienced defeat, and was suffering from the mistakes of his past. Like each one of us, he had those days when life offered nothing but confusion and despair over which way to turn. But David knew whom to go to for guidance, having previously discovered the truth he wrote in verse 10 of the same Psalm: "The LORD leads with unfailing love and faithfulness…"

It's when the fog of life is thickest that, "Show me the right path, O Lord" is the prayer that God loves to answer with a big, bright "Follow Me!" And while the fog may not clear for a time, He knows all the right roads, and His leading gives us the assurance that we'll make it through safely.

2

"Your word is a lamp to my feet and a light to my path."

Psalm 119:105

Hat. Sun cream. Sleeping bag liner. Toilet paper. Anti-bacterial hand lotion. Bug spray. Anti-malarial tablets. High-energy food bars. And so went the list of items required for our mission trip to South East Asia. There was only one item that puzzled me slightly: headlamp!

"Surely we won't be caving, will we?" I remarked to my husband, as we worked out from whom we could borrow such a piece of apparatus.

"Maybe it's dark where you're going?"

His retort reminded me that I really am a townie. To me a dark street is one where the street lamp is faulty, and the night sky is always tinged with a city-coloured-orange glow.

The first visit our little team made in Thailand was to a refugee orphanage. We arrived in bright sunshine. Overhead the most amazing blue sky was marked only by the nearby jagged mountains of Burma. Surprisingly, darkness fell quickly, tempered indoors somewhat by a single bulb dangling precariously from the ceiling, powered by a small generator. When the children had given their last hugs of the day we headed for the door.

"Headlamps, ladies!" sounded the warning. To which we dutifully stretched bands and tapes around our heads, giggling at how foolish we all looked before flicking the appropriate switch.

The lean-to door opened into an intensity of darkness I had never experienced before. Even with the faint electric light behind us I couldn't make out where the truck had been parked earlier. Thankfully our host, out in front, switched on a strong torch to let us see where the vehicle was waiting for our return, at the bottom of a steep hill.

"Heads down and point your lamp at your feet, ladies," we were instructed, "and it will give you enough light for the next step. Use your hands to balance yourself and watch out for obstacles."

Conversation stilled as we carefully picked our way along the uneven path with its rough handmade steps. The small but strong light beamed through the darkness, illuminating a foot-sized area allowing each of us onward movement. The light also picked up every little creature on our path, sending geckos and bugs of all kinds scurrying for a hiding place. But that same light made me feel secure, keeping me aware of the dangers on the path, whilst allowing me to reach the safety of the truck one step at a time.

I couldn't help but think that a larger lamp might have been better, and would have produced more light, but then it would have also been more awkward to wear. The lamp I had was adequate for the task, and its dimensions forced me to concentrate on the job in hand.

Until that night, many miles from home, I had never really understood exactly what the psalmist meant in Psalm 119:105. God's Word – the Bible – is likened to my headlamp. It gives us sufficient light for the step we need to take right now. Even though we'd love to see more of what's ahead, it is enough for the path God wants us to follow. As we read the Bible, God shows us little by little the dangers along life's journey and how the truth it contains has the power to scatter them.

Eventually, each small, illuminated step brings us to the exact place where God wants us to be. I guess that if I'd tried to make it to the truck without the headlamp that night, I might have arrived a bit bruised, if I'd arrived at all.

It makes sense to use the light at our disposal!

3

"Whenever I am afraid, I will trust in You."

Psalm 56:3

....

"What was the story about at nursery today, Bethany?"

No reply.

"Did you hear me, Bethany?" my daughter-in-law, Susie, persisted.

"Yes, mummy, but I can't tell you what it was about," the four-year-old replied, shoulders shrugged and palms upward.

"Why can't you tell me? Have you forgotten?"

"No, mummy, but I can't tell you right now," Bethany replied, head bobbing in my direction and lips firmly sealed, as if her mother should be able to work out why the subject of said story should be so secretive.

"Oh," said her astute mummy. "You don't want granny to know. Come and whisper then," she encouraged, winking at me in the process.

"I see, sweetheart," Susie nodded. "The story was about a mouse, and you didn't want to upset granny Catherine 'cause she doesn't like mice. That's very thoughtful."

Infuriated that the secret was out, Bethany threw her hands in the air. "Why did you tell her, mummy? She'll be afraid now!"

Yes, it's true. Granny Catherine is afraid of mice – not the storybook kind – but the furry, fast-moving, four-legged kind! In fact granny Catherine is so afraid of mice that the very sign of an earlier visit, or a fizzling noise that I can't explain, turns me rigid with fear. And yes, I've heard all the arguments about how they are so small and couldn't possibly do me any harm; about how they are more frightened of me than I am of them. But it is simply not true! I've never yet seen a mouse stop in its tracks when it sees me!

Fear comes into our lives in many different guises, and is much more serious than an aversion to mice or spiders or snakes. And while fear is often a healthy tool used by the body to warn us of danger and to keep us safe, it can also be a debilitating obstacle in our daily walk with God.

When the fearful prophet Habakkuk stood in disbelief, knowing that an enemy invasion was about to devastate the nation of Israel, he moved beyond his anger and confusion, and shifted his focus from fear to the reality of the God he could trust. How did he do it? He chose to call to mind all that God had done for Israel throughout their difficult history. And in the remembering, Habakkuk realized that God could deal with this difficulty too.

It always seems easier to forget than to remember. We forget how God's peace walked with us before, or how His presence was tangible when we felt so alone. You see, remembering is a choice; something we actively participate in. When fear sticks us to the floor, we choose whether to stay in its grip or to trust in the Lord, who has been with us until this point, to release us from it.

"When I am afraid, I will – *I choose to* – trust in You." (my italics). It's a choice that will never be proved wrong.

4

"The name of the LORD is a strong tower; The righteous run to it and are safe."

Proverbs 18:10

On 7 July 2005 my husband and I arrived at London's Heathrow Airport on an early flight from Belfast, to celebrate our son's graduation from the Royal College of Music, scheduled for the following day.

Our excitement quickly turned to confusion as we tried to make our way towards the exit. The place was heaving with the kind of crowd you would expect at a cup final. It was impossible to move forward, and the atmosphere was frantic with fearful tension. We managed to weave our way towards a noticeboard with a hastily scribbled announcement on it: DUE TO AN INCIDENT IN CENTRAL LONDON YOU ARE ADVISED NOT TO LEAVE THE TERMINAL BUILDING UNTIL FURTHER INFORMATION IS AVAILABLE.

We were soon to discover that a terrorist attack in several locations involving the London transport system had taken the lives of fifty-two people and injured a further 700. London was in chaos.

Ten years later a huge training exercise was carried out in the capital, involving members of the security and emergency services, to test their ability to cope should such an incident ever recur. Watching the news that evening rekindled memories of that dreadful day, but I was also fascinated by the designation given to the training exercise.

In the backrooms of officialdom someone had decided to call it: "Operation Strong Tower".

Wow! How appropriate!

Throughout history a strong tower was the place people ran to, to hide, or for protection from enemy attack. Its position and strength of construction were intended to keep its citizens safe. Often rising in stature above everything else in the locality, it was easily seen, providing a place of escape when disaster threatened.

Centuries earlier Solomon likened the name of the Lord to a strong tower; a place where the righteous could run and be safe in times of personal disaster. Then, and now, the Lord Jehovah's wide arms welcome those fleeing attack from the enemy of their souls, providing comfort for the wounded, and safety for the frail. His name always rises in stature above everything else around us. He is easily found – never hiding away from those who love Him.

How could we not run to our Strong Tower when among His names is El-Shaddai... the God who is enough; Jehovah Rophe... the Lord who heals; Jehovah Shammah... the Lord who is always there; Emmanuel... God with us?

In Christ we are safe.

So if you need to – run to Him!

5

"I have come that they may have life,
and that they may have it more abundantly."

John 10:10

....

"NO DANCING IN THE FOYER!"

These were the words that met me one Saturday morning when I arrived at a hotel to speak at a ladies' breakfast. They were written in large bold letters on two sizeable boards straddling the entrance. I couldn't help but smile at the unexpected greeting until I learned that an Irish dancing festival was being held in the main function room leading directly from the foyer.

The hotel management were making it very clear to the participants that all fun, excitement, and delight of the day were strictly to be enjoyed only by those behind the large wooden doors. Presumably

they were anxious not to disturb any of the other hotel patrons visiting for different reasons.

The leaders of our little nation, and society in general, appear to be displaying the same attitude to the Christian church today. It's alright for you Christians to have fun, experience the delight and joy of a personal relationship with Jesus Christ, as long as you keep it behind closed doors. After all, your message might offend someone. You can almost hear them

shout: "No dancing in the foyer!"

When I was leaving the hotel a couple of hours later, I passed through the foyer again. The function room door was slightly ajar and I could see the crowds of people inside experiencing something I knew nothing about. And there in the foyer was a little girl defying all the prohibitions and dancing her heart out! I couldn't help but stop for a second to watch. Her Irish dancing dress was beautiful and intricately embroidered with traditional patterns, while her curly wig bounced with every step of the jig she was practising. I for one was glad that what was hidden had been brought out from behind closed doors.

It's about time we Christians "danced in the foyer". People need to see what they are missing, and experience what they know nothing about. If they could see forgiveness first-hand, and witness joy that doesn't depend on happenings, they might be interested in this Jesus we keep so much to ourselves.

But how can they know if we don't come out from behind the closed doors of our churches, and our own fears? We might be surprised at how many people are interested in peeking through the doors we leave ajar, or the open witness of our lives.

Who's with me? Let's "dance in the foyer"!

6

"What is more pleasing to the Lord: your burnt offerings and sacrifices or your obedience to his voice? Obedience is far better than sacrifice."

1 Samuel 15:22 (NLT)

To the south of the city of Jerusalem there is a viewing point called "Abraham's Ridge". It was not originally intended to be a tourist landmark. Rather, it is believed that from this spot the great Patriarch viewed Mount Moriah, where God told him to "Take now your son, your only son Isaac, whom you love… and offer him there as a burnt offering…" (Genesis 22:2). I can't imagine what it was like for Abraham as he and his son left the ridge, walked down the winding path, through the valley, and up the steep climb to the place where God had asked him to go and do this awful thing.

But I do know this – Abraham was a man of faith.

As he and Isaac continue on their sombre journey together, they leave the servants behind. "The lad and I will go yonder and worship," Abraham tells them, "and we will come back to you" (Genesis 22:5). Did you notice the plural? "**We** will come back…"

Somehow, Abraham trusted in the promise and plan God had already revealed to him. Even if Isaac died, the Patriarch believed God could raise his son to life again (Hebrews 11:19). After all, hadn't God promised that through Isaac "all the nations of the earth shall be blessed" (Genesis 26:4)? He may not have understood God's

instruction, but he trusted in God's Word, thus making it possible to obey.

Thousands of years later, also in obedience to God's command, Jesus arrived at Mount Moriah. His view was from the east, across the Mount of Olives, towards the magnificence of Herod's Temple. Jesus' journey took Him down another winding path, past the Garden of Gethsemane, and up into the city – to the place ordained before time began, to offer Himself as the greatest sacrifice in history. Only this time, the sacrifice of an only son would not be stopped. Instead, Jesus became the "ram caught in the thicket" – the substitutionary sacrifice for our sins.

His too was a difficult journey – a journey of unflinching obedience. But one that was transformed one week later into a journey of victory as the angel declared: "He is risen!" (Mark 16:6). Jesus trusted the Father's plan.

Sometimes we are also asked to walk down a difficult road. Often the direction of this journey appears to make no sense, and may even cause pain, but as with Abraham and Jesus, God asks us to trust in His ultimate plan by walking in obedience.

Back then, Abraham's faith was credited to him as righteousness. Today, Jesus is our living Saviour, and because of Him, we are promised that: "Eye has not seen, nor ear heard, nor have entered into the heart of man the things which God has prepared for those who love Him" (1 Corinthians 2:9).

Obedience isn't always easy, but it is a journey worth taking.

7

"Dear friends, don't be surprised at the fiery trials you are going through, as if something strange were happening to you."

1 Peter 4:12 (NLT)

I love it when an author surprises me with an unexpected twist in a storyline, piquing interest and intensifying excitement.

However, that's not how the unanticipated feels when it drops into our own life story. Often the unexpected nature of adversity only adds to the pain.

After all, meeting disappointment, or even disaster, head-on isn't something we planned for. Therefore when it catches us unawares, the control we like to have of our lives is wrenched from our grasp, leaving us vulnerable and afraid. It's the kind of surprise we could well do without, as I discovered when our first child was diagnosed with a life-limiting condition. The shock that this could ever happen to us was completely devastating.

As I've grown older, and hopefully wiser, I'm now surprised that I ever thought that way in the first place. I know only too well that God never promised us a trouble-free life. Rather, He frequently declared the opposite. "Here on earth you will have many trials and sorrows," Jesus said, "but take heart, because I have overcome the world" (John 16:33 NLT).

Yet, how we initially perceive the difficulty when it arrives affects how we respond, and also affects how quickly we can start on the journey of healing with God. Unfortunately, as human beings, we seem to be hardwired in such a way that what we don't like, we don't hear, revealing a form of selective hearing.

There is no more vivid example of that than of Jesus' disciples. Startled, they ran away when their Master was arrested, kept their distance from the cross, and disbelieved the women's report when they returned from the tomb announcing that Jesus had risen from the dead! That might be perfectly understandable were it not for the fact that Jesus had already told them exactly what was going to happen in advance (Matthew 20:17–19)! But for some reason the events of Holy Week appeared to come as a complete surprise to this bunch of men who had just spent three years with the Saviour. They'd heard Jesus' words, but obviously hadn't been listening to what He was saying.

Now that our son is a father, there are some words he uses more frequently these days: "Bethany," you'll hear him say to his five-year-old, "turn on your listening ears; daddy is speaking to you."

While it might be discouraging to hear that our walk with Jesus will be fraught with difficulty, we need to turn on those listening ears, because that wasn't all Jesus said. There's much more.

"Take heart," He encourages, "because I have overcome the world."

8

"Don't copy the behaviour and customs of this world, but let God transform you into a new person by changing the way you think. Then you will know what God wants you to do, and you will know how good and pleasing and perfect his will really is."

Romans 12:2 (NLT)

At the time of writing the United Kingdom is gearing up for an election.

As in previous elections, the same old tactics are being rolled out all over again, with enough sweet talk and promises to cause political indigestion in even the most die-hard party animal. However, it is interesting to watch politicians when they appear under the media spotlight. No matter what they are asked they always manage to somehow bring the conversation back to their own agenda. They cleverly sidestep previous failures in order to highlight their successes, and churn out proposed new policies to add shine to their campaign, even if they never reach the starting block.

Let's face it; it's not only the politicians who behave in this way.

Many of our own dreams, plans, and work/home lives are ambition driven. We want to achieve a lifestyle that makes us happy, and we will work hard to reach our goals whether they are academic, financial, relational, or even philanthropic. We too have an agenda.

That same principle is easily carried with us into our spiritual lives.

In our prayer life we know exactly how we think God should answer a particular prayer. Then, when He deals with the situation differently to what we thought would be best, we are disappointed, often unwilling to accept God's answer. We've set our own agenda.

Sometimes failure hits the very things that we want to accomplish for God, and the results can be devastating. It seemed like a good idea at the time, but we didn't think of bringing God into the equation. Before long we discover that He never intended for us to be involved in the first place. We've set our own agenda.

We even dream dreams and make plans, asking God to grant them, because we are so sure they're right for us, our children, or the church. And when nothing happens, we wonder why we bother! Could it be that we've set our own agenda?

Often the problem is not our motivation, for in many cases that is good and honourable. Neither do we lack a desire to please God. The fault lies in what I call, the "me syndrome" – we just want to do it our way. We set the agenda, and then ask God to rubber-stamp it by adding His blessing.

Romans 12:2 has been life-changing for me. During a period of change in my life, I made plans that I thought were good and wholesome, and asked God to bless them. Instead of answering my requests He tormented me with these words, which I've paraphrased: *"Don't live like everyone else, Catherine. The rat race isn't for you. Let me transform you. Let me change the way you think. If you do, you'll not only know my plans for you, you'll discover they are perfect!"*

Truthfully, it wasn't an easy decision to make, but it was the right one. There's only room for one pilot in any cockpit! And on the days I find it difficult to listen to what God says, I read Romans 12:2 again, and prop up the little card on my desk that shouts at me:

"PURSUE GOD'S AGENDA!"

9

"The LORD is like a father to his children, tender and compassionate to those who fear him."

Psalm 103:13 (NLT)

I was driving along the busy A26 one Saturday when I noticed two cyclists not too far ahead on the road. *They're brave,* I thought, sensing the impatience of some drivers at having to slow down.

The cyclists were easy to spot, dressed in the appropriately brightly coloured gear for their activity, and seated atop very expensive-looking bicycles. But the thing that caught my attention was the age difference of the sporting companions. One was a fit-looking young man, while the other was only a child: a boy around ten years old. Father and son, I reckoned.

The father cycled slightly ahead of the boy, keeping to the right of his precious charge, thereby shielding him from the danger of passing traffic. Every so often the young man would glance around, smiling proudly at his prodigy.

The son kept his front wheel aligned to the back wheel of his father's bicycle, his eyes constantly focused not on the traffic, but on his father ever so slightly ahead. As I passed them I noticed the boy biting his bottom lip nervously. Yet, underneath his blue safety helmet, I could see his eyes were filled with an obvious look of excitement. The fear of danger was moderated by the presence of one whom he so evidently trusted.

As they faded from my rear-view mirror I imagined the breakfast table talk of tactics to employ when cycling in traffic… of the boy's questions, and the father's responses. Especially the promise verbalized: "I'll lead the way, son. All you have to do is to stay close to me. I'll keep you safe."

Afterwards, I couldn't help but smile as I thought of the story they would be able to tell when they arrived home!

Throughout Scripture God refers to Himself as a father to His children, "tender and compassionate to those who fear him" (Psalm 103:13 NLT). There are even times when our heavenly Father asks us to swing our legs over the bar and follow Him into dangerous traffic. It can be a nerve-wracking experience, but then He always promises to go with us, leading the way and making the risk worthwhile.

And just imagine what a story we will have to tell when we get home!

10

"But let patience have its perfect work, that you may be perfect and complete, lacking nothing."

James 1:4

Everyone who visited the Temple in Jerusalem knew Simeon.

When mothers and fathers brought their baby boys to fulfil the requirements of the Jewish law, Simeon was always hovering nearby. He was the old man of the Temple, righteous and respected, and a man with a story to tell. Word had it that Simeon had had a divine revelation that he wouldn't die until he had seen the Lord's Messiah (Luke 2:25–26).

And so blessing little children became Simeon's daily delight. But as the months passed into years nothing happened. And with the passage of time the faithful probably humoured the old man's claims. After all, Jehovah had been silent for four hundred years. Why would He reveal Himself now? And to an old man?

But Simeon was patient. He believed God. And his waiting was rewarded.

"So when Mary and Joseph came to present the baby Jesus to the Lord as the law required, Simeon was there" (Luke 2:27–28 NLT).

Simeon was there! The old man was in his place.

I wonder if he ever doubted God's promise? Did he ever feel foolish turning up at the Temple day after weary day? Did his patience ever waver as he looked into the faces of a multitude of babies, only to realize time after time that this wasn't the one? I don't know. But I know this; the old man of the Temple waited until God fulfilled His promise. He never gave up. Instead, Simeon's patience provided him with the opportunity to meet Jesus: to hold the Son of God in his frail arms – to welcome Israel's promised Messiah.

"Lord, now I can die in peace!" he announced. "As you promised me, I have seen the Saviour you have given to all people" (Luke 2:29–31 NLT).

The waiting was worth it!

Are you any good at waiting?

Somehow, sitting in God's waiting room is just no fun. His timing never seems to work in synchronization with ours. We want everything yesterday, while He asks us to wait. To wait for that answer to prayer; to wait for that promise to be fulfilled; to wait for that prodigal to return. Yet there are few of us who can claim to have patience hardwired into our personality. Waiting is undoubtedly one of life's most difficult tasks.

But what would happen if we gave up waiting? What if we doubted His promises in our lives? What if we were not in our place when God's answer or His promise arrived?

Think what we might miss!

11

"Let us strip off every weight that slows us down, especially the sin that so easily hinders our progress. And let us run with endurance the race God has set before us. We do this by keeping our eyes on Jesus, whom our faith depends on from start to finish."

Hebrews 12:1–2 (NLT)

I've always dreamed of learning to ski. But there's a problem – I'm afraid of heights. And since ski lifts are required to get you to the top of the slopes, skiing is not an option for me.

But it doesn't stop me watching the professionals speed down the steep mountain slopes, from the comfort of my armchair. The sight is breathtaking. Competitors in the Downhill and Super-G events take part in races that are both difficult and dangerous. Perhaps, surprisingly, we can learn much from the skier that will help us run our own race of life, as the writer to the Hebrews encourages us to do.

Just like the skier at the start of the race, we too must pass through the narrow gate (Matthew 7:13). For when we are called to repentance we dare not delay.

In order to make progress we need to head in the right direction and steer between the flagged gates – flags God has set in His Word to keep us on course – encouragement, promises, rebukes, and the help of the Holy Spirit. How sad it is to watch a skier lose the prize because he veered off course! If we are to finish the race we too must stay between the flags.

Each skier starting at the top of the mountain knows there is a danger of falling, and with that fall they risk injury or even death. So they do everything in their power to keep upright, streamlining their bodies, not merely for speed, but to stop them crashing out of the race. They carry nothing that might hinder them or stop them from finishing. They don't want to see DNF written beside their name on the leader board. God's Word warns us to strip off everything, especially any sin that could slow down our progress or, worse still, cause us to fall.

Skiing requires great courage as the competitor battles the steep twists and turns of the course. As we hurtle down dangerous paths in life's race it's good to remember that we are "kept by the power of God" (1 Peter 1:5). He has promised to keep us upright.

What keeps the skiers on track? Why don't they give up? They focus on the finishing line! They know it's ahead and so they keep on going.

How can we reach the finishing line of the race that is set before us? "We do this by keeping our eyes on Jesus," the writer to the Hebrews tells us, "whom our faith depends on from start to finish" (Hebrews 12:2 NLT).

And when we slide over the line, what a celebration awaits us!

12

"Since you were precious in My sight, you have been honoured, and I have loved you."

Isaiah 43:4

....

"Oh Bethany! I have an earworm!"

Looking across the room rather startled at the thought of a creepy-crawly attacking my daughter-in-law, I was surprised to hear Bethany reply: "What song is it, mummy?"

A guessing game quickly ensued as to which of the songs from the movie Frozen was on a perpetual loop in Susie's head, which is apparently the correct definition of earworm – not the wriggly invertebrate I was imagining!

It happens to us all at times, doesn't it? You waken up one morning with a song that plays constantly on repeat all day. It can be infuriating. For some reason our mind hits the replay button again and again, and it is hard to switch off that particular song or tune. Psychologists tell us that it is usually related to something significant in our lives – a celebration or wedding song – or involving a topic we've been spending a lot of time thinking about.

On one such occasion I couldn't get an old hymn out of my mind, in spite of the fact that I hadn't sung it in a long time. The earworm had struck, but I had a sneaking suspicion that I knew why. I had been speaking in the previous days about how precious we are to God:

how very deeply He loves each one of us. Yet it seems to be a difficult truth for some people to grasp.

I frequently meet women whose experience of love is that it is something to be earned; you have to be worthy of it. They believe that love is a response, if you like, to behaving in a certain way. It is frequently used as a reward, and never given for free... just for being me.

More often than not, women have shared with me their experiences of love lost through affairs, divorce, a difference of opinion, an argument, or more permanently, because of death. Sadly circumstances reinforce a belief that they are unlovable. Others have been viciously abused in spite of the offender avowing their love for them.

Is it any wonder Isaiah's words are so precious, or that I don't mind the particular earworm playing on and on in my head? Because the old hymn reminds me of God's "love that wilt not let me go"

... even if I mess up

... even if I don't meet other people's expectations – or my own

... even if I don't always get it right.

God loves me for me. No need to jump through hoops. He sees me as precious and honoured. There is nothing I can do that will make Him love me any less. His love cannot be earned. It is freely, simply, and magnificently given. No strings attached.

Play on, earworm!

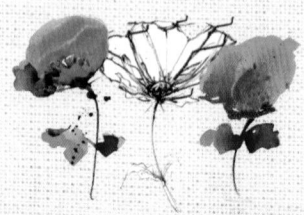

13

"And you shall know the truth, and the truth shall make you free."

John 8:32

....

"But you know that's not true!" I blurted out, almost spraying the face of the young woman sitting across the table from me. "How can you possibly believe that?"

"It's true to me," came the quiet response, muffled further by choked cries that refused to stay where an attempt had been made to tether them. "I'm just a horrible person... to look at... to be with. I don't even like myself, so why should others like me?"

Poor self-image, compounded by difficult personal circumstances, had become her prison; a dark place with no apparent hope of escape. But I knew this woman. I knew her big heart, had personal experience of her love and her walk with God.

"God doesn't love me anymore," she continued. "I don't know how long it's been since He answered any of my prayers."

I wanted to shake her, to tell her to stop talking nonsense, to add my clichés to hers – tell her that she should stop believing the devil's lies! But thankfully, God kept my tongue in my mouth, and I listened, feeling the overwhelming darkness of her despair.

Later, we watched the waves roll in and I knew it was time to speak: "What you said isn't true, you know."

"Which part?"

"All of it."

And so it was her turn to listen, as we gently explored together what truth is – God's truth. The truth displayed in the person of His Son, the truth of His unconditional love for us, the truth of His eternal plan for us whatever our circumstances. And the liberating truth that God has no favourites. The slim are no more loved than the overweight, or the able-bodied no more than the disabled, or the financially successful than the person struggling between paydays.

Somehow the sight of the waves lapping the stony shore was God's visual aid as we thought on these things. After all, the sea always reaches the shore whether it lands on golden sand or stony coastline; the wideness of His compassion relentlessly finding a way to reach where we stand.

To Thomas, for whom doubt seemed a way of life, Jesus made it simple in John 14:6 when He said: "I am the way, the truth, and the life." Thomas, like each one of us, had to choose whether to believe "the Truth" and accept freedom from his constant uncertainty, or not to believe and continue in the darkness of despair.

Today, as every day, the prison door of our misconceptions gapes in front of us, opened wide by the truth that longs to set us free. The question is – are we prepared to walk through it?

14

"But we are citizens of heaven, where the Lord Jesus Christ lives. And we are eagerly waiting for him to return as our Saviour. He will take our weak, mortal bodies and change them into glorious bodies like his own, using the same power with which he will bring everything under his control."

Philippians 3:20–21 (NLT)

Airports are fascinating places.

Initially they carry equal amounts of delight and dismay when we arrive at the terminal building. The excitement of a trip is mixed with the sight of long queues at check-in, followed by long queues at security, and – even if you think you've been clever enough to check-in online – long queues at bag-drop!

Clock-watching, finger-tapping, stress-inducing waiting. It can dampen your enthusiasm for travel, or catastrophically cause you to miss your flight altogether.

Yet once you pick up your phone, belt, shoes, coat, coins, and anything else that might make the scanner ping, from the plastic tray, your heart rate slows and you enter an altogether different world. A world where citizens of many nations mix, mingle, and wait a little bit longer until they hear those magic words: "Some-world Airways are pleased to announce the departure of flight…"

And you're off! With passport and boarding pass in hand to ensure the final barrier is crossed, you are finally allowed to board the flight that will take you to your destination.

Yet, sometimes it's arrivals that fill me with dread, especially in a foreign country. I'd love to be heading for the passport control of the host nation, with words like "US Citizens this way", rather than the snaking lines of foreigners soon to be scrutinized by suspicious immigration officers. Their intense questioning always makes me aware of the fact that I am not one of their citizens, and frequently I get the impression that they'd rather I hadn't come!

Travelling home is so very different. As a citizen of the UK I head for the sign that says "EU citizens this way", and with a cursory glance at my passport, and sometimes even a smile, I'm waved on… no questions asked. And I'm home.

Life can be so much like the airport at times, frustrated by waiting and feeling as if you don't belong in a society increasingly keen to reject God's law. Paul hit the nail on the head when he explained to the young believers at Philippi, and to us today, that we are citizens of Heaven. The good news being that airports are places of transition; temporary stops on life's journey.

Too often we feel our weakness and frailty, accompanied by a sense of discomfort at all that is going on around us personally and nationally. Yet one day we will go home to where Jesus lives. And as citizens of Heaven we won't need to go through passport control because He will already have taken "our weak mortal bodies and change[d] them into glorious bodies like his own."

What a thought to push back the darkness of the here-and-now. We're just passing through. Heaven is our home! And our welcome there will be huge.

15

"Behold, I am coming quickly! Hold fast what you have, that no one may take your crown."

Revelation 3:11

Once upon a time there were seven churches. Each one a bright jewel in the crown of early Christendom, bringing spiritual light into the darkness of their separate locations.

In fact, they all did so well that God sent individual letters to each of the churches, to commend them for their faithfulness in spite of suffering, together with their hard work, loyalty, love, service, and endurance through much opposition. Wow! How amazing is that? A direct communiqué from Heaven! I'm sure their chests swelled as the words were read out.

But wait, that's not the end of the story. Truth be told, this is no fairy tale. It's the reality of seven churches described in the book of Revelation. Only two of the seven could continue to bask in the commendation of God. For the other five churches, God had more to say. And it wasn't pretty.

"Nevertheless, I have this against you," He went on to say to each of the remaining five, with a cringe factor of seismic proportions.

I wonder did their smiles disappear, or their heads hang low as they listened to the accusations of the One who had given His Son for them? Were any tears shed as He pointed out the sinful practices of idolatry, immorality, heresy, backsliding, and apathy that they were tolerating within the church, and their own lives? Yet even in this God offered mercy for repentance; reward for perseverance. But we don't read of repentance. Instead the light went out.

Having stood in Ephesus, the home of one of these churches, I was especially saddened to read of how they had been accused of "leaving their first love" (Revelation 2:4). How did that happen to this vibrant church – this community of Jesus' followers? We are not told. My guess is that their problem mirrors much of ours today. It happened little by little, without their noticing it.

How easy it is for us to allow that first fiery passion for our Saviour to be diluted with the "everyday" of our lives. Slowly, the time we make in our busy lives for Jesus results in a nodding acquaintance with Him, rather than that required for "him whom my soul loves" (Song of Solomon 3:4 NIV). Perish the thought that we could so effortlessly drift from the Ephesian problem – leaving our first love – to the Laodicean one: becoming so lukewarm that we make God sick!

Perhaps like me, your longing is to be like the Smyrnans or the Philadelphians, while praying that God will keep us off the slippery slope to Laodicea. But I've discovered that God's answer to that prayer has been bounced back into my court, placing that responsibility firmly with me.

The words of Revelation 3:11 ring loud in my ears: "Hold fast what you have, that no one may take your crown."

16

"Entreat me not to leave you, Or to turn back from following after you; For wherever you go, I will go; And wherever you lodge, I will lodge; Your people shall be my people, And your God, my God."

Ruth 1:16

2015 saw my husband and me celebrate thirty-eight years of marriage, while our son and daughter-in-law reached their first decade together. Topping all of that, my parents have enjoyed all of sixty-five years as man and wife. Between the three generations we have clocked up 113 years of married life!

Yet, marriage is about much more than statistics, isn't it?

It's about love given and received; being able to say sorry; keeping promises – even the one that says: "in sickness and in health"; building up rather than tearing down; weathering the storms of life together. And I've discovered that it can all be summarized in one word.

Commitment.

It's a discipline that involves total, selfless dedication – not merely in relationships, but in every area of our lives. Can we be trusted? Is our word worth anything? Does what I do match what I say?

Ruth's commitment to her widowed mother-in-law centuries ago is legendary. She promised to go with Naomi, live with her, and even to follow Naomi's God. Was she committed? Did she follow through? Yes, a thousand times, even through poverty and difficulty. But her commitment, though costly, produced great rewards, for there in the genealogy of Christ, recorded in Matthew's Gospel (1:5), is Ruth's name.

In the emotion of the moment, when the band strikes up in a big conference, it's easy to sing with gusto: "I have decided to follow Jesus!" But when following Jesus becomes uncomfortable, have we got what it takes for the "no turning back" line of the old chorus?

How does commitment figure in our walk with God?

17

"Concerning this thing I pleaded with the Lord three times that it might depart from me. And He said to me, 'My grace is sufficient for you, for My strength is made perfect in weakness.'"

2 Corinthians 12:8–9

Diphylleia grayi are beautiful white woodland blossoms.

They grow in the cooler regions of Japan, China, and on the slopes of the Appalachian mountain range in America. On first inspection they are pretty, yes, but not spectacular, as they bloom from the centre of bright green foliage. The small white petals present a somewhat ordinary look, tinged with frailty. They certainly don't appear able to withstand a storm.

But, the first lesson you learn from diphylleia grayi is that looks can deceive, for it's when the rain comes that these little flowers come into their own. As the delicate petals are pounded with water from above, you are convinced that they'll never survive nature's onslaught. The water quickly removes the white colouring, rendering the flower completely translucent. Every tiny vein is pronounced; the delicate edging shimmers; nothing is hidden. You can see straight through the flower to the greenery below, hence its common name: skeleton flower.

Is it dying? you wonder, as the rain continues its devastating blows.

Quite the opposite in fact. For in its most vulnerable-looking state the little plant is gaining strength, and when the rain stops and it dries out, it reverts to the white woodland flower it was before. For a brief period of time it looked as if it couldn't possibly survive. Although rendered defenceless and exposed, the beating results in transparent beauty – its survival causing us to gasp in admiration.

So when the rain beats us down let's remember that Paul affirms that in Christ, weakness is transformed into strength.

18

"Fear not, for I am with you; Be not dismayed, for I am your God. I will strengthen you, Yes, I will help you, I will uphold you with My righteous right hand."

Isaiah 41:10

Fear is the kind of darkness that paralyzes. Its grip exerts a destructive stranglehold in many areas of our lives, particularly on our perception. With weed-like growth, we see it as unstoppable and unconquerable, but one of the things fear does best is to lie to us.

It doesn't have to be this way.

I have frequently heard it said that there are 366 "Fear nots" in the Bible. It's lovely to think that God whispers His peace to our hearts every day of the year, including a leap year, but to be honest I haven't checked.

But I do know this, that every time I hear God say those words to my heart it causes me to examine why I am afraid, and to trust God for the promises He adds.

Maybe some of these reassurances will help with whatever causes your heart to tremble today.

Feeling you can't cope: "For I, the LORD your God, will hold your right hand, Saying to you, 'Fear not, I will help you'" (Isaiah 41:13).

Needing guidance: "And the LORD, He is the One who goes before you. He will be with you, He will not leave you nor forsake you; do not fear nor be dismayed" (Deuteronomy 31:8).

Feeling the needles of opposition: "Do not fear the reproach of men, Nor be afraid of their insults" (Isaiah 51:7).

Struggling in Christian service: "Do not fear or be dismayed; tomorrow go out against them, for the LORD is with you" (2 Chronicles 20:17b).

I could go on and on. God understands our human frailty, especially in respect of fear. That's why He tells us so often not to fear, bolstering what seems impossible with His enabling for whatever produces the fear in the first place.

Terrified by the dream he had seen and all the ramifications that would follow, the prophet Daniel was visited by God who instantly spoke into his fear. "O man greatly beloved, fear not!" God said. "Peace be to you; be strong, yes, be strong!" (Daniel 10:19).

As we hear God's compassionate words to our hearts today, may we respond like Daniel: "Let my lord speak, for you have strengthened me" (verse 19).

19

"Yes, I have loved you with an everlasting love; Therefore with lovingkindness I have drawn you."

Jeremiah 31:3

During my work life I have had the privilege of delivering over fifty babies. In each of those births I discovered the amazing lesson of how pain can produce such a perfect gift of love.

I thought nothing could top that wonderful feeling of being so actively involved in the arrival of a new little life – until that is, my own children arrived! Two daughters and one son later, I can verify that there is nothing to compare with the thrill motherhood brings.

Recently, with the birth of Daniel David, I have now also had the privilege of holding two grandchildren in my arms, and both of them have stolen my heart.

During our first visit to greet our new little grandson, I commented to Susie, my daughter-in-law, how when you have your first child you can never imagine loving another little person as much as the one you already have – until the next one is placed in your arms. It's only then that you realize the mammoth capabilities of the human heart to love more than one person with the exact same depth of feeling. How lovely to watch our son's precious little family of three become four – adding a mere 7lb 11oz of human flesh but a mountain of love.

How is it possible to love in this way?

Because, as we read in the book of Genesis, we are made in the image of God – and God is love. Just as our son Paul is bursting with fatherly love for his newborn son, yet continues to dote on his darling daughter, so God's heart explodes with love for all of His children.

And He even loves those described as unlovely, for "while we were still sinners, Christ died for us" (Romans 5:8). Now that is love I don't deserve, but God graciously gives it anyway.

As we have welcomed little Daniel David into our family, and into our hearts, I can't help but be overwhelmed that we too are loved "with an everlasting love" by the One who has us in His heart... and has inscribed our names on His wounded hands.

20

"Death and life are in the power of the tongue, And those who love it will eat its fruit."

Proverbs 18:21

I wonder what thoughts came to mind as you read those words?

Did you automatically think of a caustic verbal bashing you received from someone? Or perhaps it was the sly little innuendos thrown your way when a group of friends met for coffee. Could it have been a thoughtless comment about your dress, or the way you carry out a particular task, which pierced like a knife?

A modern translation of the first phrase in this verse is often given as "words have power". But its simplicity fails to emphasize the ambiguity of that power – for both *death* and *life* are held within the influence of the tongue. The words we choose to use have power, yes, but power to exert extreme opposite effects on those who receive them.

Simply put, our words can destroy, or they can encourage.

With misuse, what we say can cause deep pain, sometimes with devastating consequences. Too frequently relationships fall apart, reputations are ruined, and lives are damaged, all by thoughtless talk. And while it's easy to point the finger at someone who has harmed us in this way, we ourselves need to watch how we use our words.

Somehow *death* words are much more keenly remembered than *life* words. Words of compliment or encouragement appear to dissolve

59

more easily from our memory, like ice on a hot day. Could that be because we so rarely hear them?

Earlier in Proverbs 18 we are reminded that: "A person's words can be life-giving water" (verse 4 NLT). Imagine – a kind word; an acknowledgment; a greeting; a thank you; a commendation – can refresh a parched heart. Now that really is powerful!

It sounds almost too simple, doesn't it?

However, the challenge for us is to form the habit of choosing to use words of *life* rather than *death* in our interaction with others. Let's take seriously the advice Paul gives in his first letter to the Thessalonian believers: "So encourage each other and build each other up" (5:11 NLT).

Go on, try it – give away a compliment today – and be blessed by the smile it produces!

21

"Seeing their faith, Jesus said to the paralyzed man, 'My child, your sins are forgiven.'"

Mark 2:5 (NLT)

It's great to have friends, isn't it? Especially the kind who see what you need, and then get on and do something about it.

Today's verse is taken from a fantastic story in Mark 2:1–12 that you might like to read for yourself. It covers so much about everyday things – sickness, friendship, initiative, ingenuity, and even miracles! In a nutshell, a paralyzed man is carried on a stretcher to Jesus, and Jesus heals him.

But wait, I've left a whole lot out, especially the bit about his friends not being able to get into the crowded house and digging a hole in the roof to lower their friend down through it! I told you it was good! Mind you, they must have been both puzzled and disappointed with what they heard from their rooftop position. "Your sins are forgiven," the Rabbi said, rather than, "you are healed." All their effort for this?

The friends had made a common mistake. They thought the man's most important need was to walk again. It was something they could see, and something that was impacting his life in dreadful ways. They had heard that Jesus was a miracle worker, and believed without a shadow of a doubt that if they could get their friend to Him he would be healed.

In fact it was because of that very faith that Jesus spoke those words of forgiveness in the first place. The friends wanted their companion to have a life free from pain and suffering. A magnanimous gesture indeed, but incomplete – for Jesus could do so much more for the man than his friends ever dreamed.

Like each one of us, the man had a sin-problem. Unlike the temporary problem of sickness, sin is a problem with devastating eternal consequences, hence Jesus' desire to deal with it as a matter of priority. Forgiveness was far and away the man's greatest need, and something only Jesus could do for him. And a short time later the friends got what they had originally come for. After all, Jesus never does anything by halves.

"Stand up," Jesus told the paralyzed man. "Take your mat, and go home, because you are healed!" (Mark 2:11 NLT).

I am so grateful for friends who sacrificially helped us during the years when we were caring for our two profoundly disabled daughters. Often they recognized what was needed and just got on and did it, relieving us of many practical chores, and lifting us up when we felt we couldn't go on. Friends like that are precious indeed.

But I will be eternally grateful for the one friend who, when I was fourteen years old, took me to a place where I heard that I needed to be forgiven of my sin – a need that surpassed all others in my life. And in that place I met with Jesus.

The supreme task we have as friends is to introduce those we know and love to Jesus – to help them prioritize their greatest need as that of forgiveness. Not easy. There may be a few "tiles to loosen" on the way, but Jesus will reward our faith!

Amazingly, we don't even need a friend to bring us. Jesus simply waits for the prayer of repentance and faith, and works the miracle of forgiveness in our hearts!

Didn't I tell you earlier that miracles are an everyday occurrence!

22

"He went a little farther and fell on His face, and prayed, saying, 'O My Father, if it is possible, let this cup pass from Me; nevertheless, not as I will, but as You will.'"

Matthew 26:39

I find the whole store loyalty card scheme rather amusing.

The principle behind it being, that if you sign up to the scheme with a particular store or company then you receive benefits in return for your loyalty to them. That is, of course, if you actually spend enough money to accrue the points required for vouchers or discount. These companies want you to stay, and shop, with them, and they address you in communications as a "loyal" or "valued" customer.

However, the reason I find the scheme amusing becomes obvious the moment I open my purse. Because there, for all the world to see, is my growing collection of loyalty cards. The presence of so many of these little plastic items diminishes the impact of the word loyalty, doesn't it!

In fact, the whole concept of loyalty appears to be a difficult one for us twenty-first-century folk to grasp. The dictionary definition encompasses words like faithful, devoted, reliable, promising an allegiance to someone or something. Clarification, if it is needed, that loyalty actually requires something from me. A point not well illustrated by the contents of my purse.

Evidence abounds that it's not only commerce that suffers from our unwillingness to choose loyalty as a daily discipline. Marriage; friendship; employment; church membership; volunteering; and even our walk with Christ, can be too easily damaged, or even destroyed, if we feel that the personal cost is more than we are willing to pay.

Yet contrary to the message we are fed from many directions, life is not all about me.

Jesus turned that train of thought on its head when He said: "If anyone desires to come after Me, let him deny himself, and take up his cross daily, and follow Me" (Luke 9:23).

Loyalty. This is what it takes to truly follow Jesus – lives demonstrating consistent faithfulness and devotion, while also promising our undivided allegiance. Tall order – yes! Easy – no! But then Jesus never asks from us what He Himself has not done for us.

"Not as I will, but as You will" (Matthew 26:39).

Surely, that is the kind of loyalty that is life-defining!

23

"Create in me a clean heart, O God. Renew a right spirit within me."

Psalm 51:10 (NLT)

"Do you realize that it's been two years since your last appointment?"

I'm glad I don't blush easily as I certainly felt embarrassed at the dental receptionist's words. I mumbled a few limp excuses and went to sit in the waiting room like a scolded child on the "naughty-step".

A few days later I visited the optician and wanted to crawl away when a comment was made about my previous eye test having been three years ago! Thankfully when I sat in the hairdresser's chair the following day I felt a little smugger as it had only been a month since I'd graced her with my presence.

Yes, it was one of those "catching-up" weeks. I was finally finding time to do some of the things that I'd put on the back burner while I'd been busy with what I like to call the more important things in life. Whilst trying to make excuses for my rather shocking omissions, I reminded myself of the previous calamitous year, with so much family sickness that it was far from amusing.

However, the fact we were already into the fourth month of the new year and I was only just getting to those things that should have had my attention ages ago, rendered my excuses more than a tad lame.

And after all my endeavours to make amends, no one even noticed my new glasses!

A short time later, I was deeply challenged by the words of Psalm 51:10 when it was read by someone at the church's early-morning prayer meeting. "Create in me a clean heart, O God," the psalmist said, "and renew a steadfast spirit within me." The words were made more potent because David used them after he had been challenged, and forgiven, over his act of adultery with Bathsheba.

It's one thing eventually getting the outside sorted out, I heard my Master whisper in my ear, *but I'm not particularly bothered about that.* And as I let His Word wash over my soul, I realized that I could only have a clean heart if He created it in me. For that I need to stay close while He does the necessary work – however busy I may be.

And I wondered, if God kept a record of attendance at those spiritual appointments so necessary for my life as His child, would He be disappointed in me, or would I have to slink away in embarrassment?

24

"And if anyone says to you, 'Why are you doing this?' say, 'The Lord has need of it,' and immediately he will send it here."

Mark 11:3

We all like to feel needed.

It's frustrating to watch people around you engage in some useful activity, while you stand on the sidelines with both arms the same length. It can make you feel pretty useless. Yet, sometimes we have to let those who know what they are doing simply get on with it. Which is why I stay well away from the kitchen during a church event!

However, we all have different natural abilities, as well as being endowed with a variety of spiritual gifting. The apostle Paul details the diversity of gifts in 1 Corinthians 12, ranging from apostles and pastors right 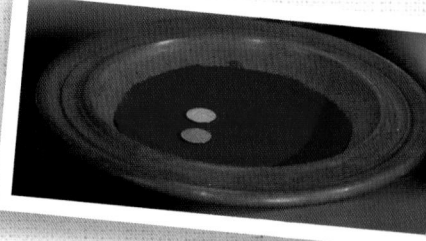 through to believers who have the gift of "helps".

Quite a difference, eh? Well actually, no. Apart from love being cited as the greatest gift (1 Corinthians 13:13), there is no hierarchy of gifts listed in the Bible. Rather, each one is of equal importance when used for God's glory.

Jesus commended the widow's giving of two small coins above the riches of others in the Temple offering (Mark 12:41–44). The boy's lunch was used to miraculous effect when placed in the saviour's hands (John 6:9–13). During the desert wanderings, gifts of goat's hair or badger skin were needed in the construction of the tabernacle, as much as gold and precious stones. God made it possible for everyone, rich or poor, skilled craftsman or common labourer, to have an equal opportunity to bless God's heart by contributing whatever they could.

There was only one requirement – that of a willing heart.

"From everyone who gives it *willingly with his heart*," God said to Moses, "you shall take My offering" (Exodus 25:2, my italics).

God does not measure how much we have or what we can do, but He is interested in the willingness of our heart to offer both for His glory. Down through history, the God of Heaven has chosen to work through the human instrument, which is why we should never feel surplus-to-requirements as one of His children.

In the verse at the top of the page, what was it that the Lord needed?

A donkey! Yes, it really was a donkey. He needed it to ride into Jerusalem that first Palm Sunday morning. No noble steed for the Son of God. Instead the Messiah was glorified riding on top of an insignificant donkey.

Now if God can use a donkey, imagine how He can be glorified in us... especially when what we offer comes from a willing heart.

25

"So is my word that goes out from my mouth: It will not return to me empty, but will accomplish what I desire and achieve the purpose for which I sent it."

Isaiah 55:11 (NIV)

The scene filling the screen was stunning!

The forest greens of jungle vegetation shrouded the beautiful mountain terrain like heavy curtains hiding secrets. As the camera zoomed in, a short grassy runway came into view. Suddenly there were tribal people everywhere, dancing, singing, and shaking the ground beneath with excitement as a tiny white plane appeared on the horizon.

Minutes later, we in the audience watched as the Mission Aviation Fellowship plane landed precariously, its wings extending to the very edge of the narrow grass landing strip. The cheers of the crowd reached fever pitch on that limited mountaintop expanse, as boxes were unloaded from the small aircraft.

What was it that evoked such a reaction in these people, normally hidden from the rest of the world in their secluded mountain home?

The Hula people of Papua were receiving the first copies of the Bible in their own language. And they were ecstatic! It was December 2014, and while I have four translations of my English Bible sitting beside me on my desk, and another few dozen available to me online, these dear people were receiving God's Word in printed form for the very first time.

Tears rolled down dusty cheeks and rib-squeezing hugs were exchanged, as the missionary who had worked for years on this translation placed the precious book into many hands! It was an emotional scene to watch. You'd have thought these dear people had been given treasure.

As a matter of fact they had.

For God's Word is described in Psalm 19:10 as "fine gold" to enrich our lives, and "honey and the honeycomb" to nourish us completely.

In addition, we are told that the Word will accomplish what God desires for our lives – challenge; rebuke; forgiveness; love; reconciliation; comfort; healing; direction; joy… and much, much more.

Of course, this is dependent on whether or not we read it, which in turn depends on just how precious we believe the Bible to be. If we get that wrong, then we are burying gold!

26

"Keep on asking, and you will be given what you ask for. Keep on looking, and you will find. Keep on knocking, and the door will be opened."

Matthew 7:7 (NLT)

Irritating, isn't it? The constant moaning of a child in the supermarket, badgering its accompanying adult for something it wants. The persistent whining makes you glad that the child causing all the embarrassment isn't yours, while smugly you tell yourself there is no way you would ever give in to such behaviour!

Jesus' words in Matthew's Gospel might almost give the impression that we are encouraged to be like cantankerous children; that pester-prayer will get you what you want from God. Not so. God is simply checking our persistence. Whether we are asking, seeking, or knocking on a closed door, our heavenly Father tests our tenacity to discover His will in the very thing causing us to seek His face.

This verse cannot be separated from Jesus' teaching on prayer that we find in other places in these Sermon-on-the-Mount chapters. We are reminded not to pray like the hypocrite, or while harbouring sin in our hearts, but rather to focus on honouring God's name, doing God's will, and making the Kingdom of God our primary concern (Matthew 6).

Once all of this is understood, the keeping-on of asking, seeking, knocking, loses the whining nature of self-seeking desire, and is transformed into the request of a mature child, longing for the Father's response to their heartfelt cries.

What is causing you to persevere in prayer? Whatever it is, remember whatever weighs on your heart, undoubtedly weighs on His heart too.

Our Father-God may need to change our hearts as we ask, and His answers may not be what we expect, but He does want us to keep on praying.

While you pray, remember this: "The earnest prayer of a righteous person has great power and wonderful results" (James 5:16 NLT).

Don't give up!

27

"He will remove all of their sorrows, and there will be no more death or sorrow or crying or pain. For the old world and its evils are gone forever. And the one sitting on the throne said, 'Look, I am making all things new!'"

Revelation 21:4–5 (NLT)

We read books for different reasons: some for pleasure and others for instruction.

My publisher once advised me, as a novice writer, to read a particular author in order that I might learn more about the craft of writing from her. The book I chose delivered exactly what was headlined on the cover: a story of "Love and war. Murder and mercy. Betrayal and forgiveness."

I couldn't put it down. Every page dared me to turn to the next one, in spite of the fact that the story made me weep and caused me to inwardly churn in horror, and even disbelief. You see, large chunks of it dealt with the story of a Holocaust survivor. I was challenged by her story to walk in the darkness, whilst at the same time being touched by tender moments of light, laughter, and love.

But it is what the book teaches about memory that impacted me most. For the pages of *The Storyteller* by Jodi Picoult remind me that memory has great power: power to paralyze, demoralize, destroy, discourage, and cause pain. Pain that returns us to a state of

helplessness that we would prefer never to revisit.

Is it any wonder that many have gone to great lengths to try to bury dark moments, or even years, within the prison of their subconcious minds?

Yet memory has other powers too. It has the power to allow little bubbles of light to float to the surface of our difficulties and pierce the darkness of that prison. It was memories of playful banter with a much-loved father; the smell of bread baking in the oven at their bakery; the touch of that first stolen kiss on her teenage lips, that broke through the horror of the character Minka's living nightmare to enable her to keep living when it seemed she would not.

There are times when I wake in the darkness and visit places I do not like to go, like when the squeal of an oxygen monitor sent Philip and me careering into our little Joy's bedroom on the night that she died.

Memory takes me to those last moments when I told her it was okay to go – that Jesus was waiting with a new body for her: to the warmth of her little frame in my arms for the last time, and the pictures of pain etched on the faces of her darling daddy and devoted brother.

But returning to that difficult place means that I can also experience the bubbles of light that broke through the darkness of that sad night, as the light shone through the silk butterfly beside her bed, reminding me of the change that only death can bring in the hands of a merciful God. And with it the promise is repeated that one day He will "make all things new" (Revelation 21:5).

"You see, Minka," the little girl's father said in the book, "Anything is possible. Even the most terrible beast might one day be a distant memory."

To all the Minkas of this world I would add… not *might*… but **will**.

With the passing of the years I have discovered that light is best appreciated in dark places. As long as we determine to walk in the Light He gives, it will dispel our darkness, bringing hope and, yes, in time, even joy once more. So, it's okay to remember.

28

"Bear one another's burdens, and so fulfil the law of Christ."

Galatians 6:2

As the pastor of our church, my husband chooses a motto text for each year, encouraging the congregation to memorize it, meditate on its principles, and then live out its truth. Today's verse was our text for 2015.

These are very challenging words, especially in these ultra-busy days in which we live. Yet they have the power to help us bring light into the dark places of people's lives, particularly those with whom we rub shoulders each day.

Our response to this command can be worked out in different ways. We can offer practical and financial help to those in need, and some are more able to do that than others. But all of us can be involved in bearing the burdens of others through prayer.

No one demonstrated the power of this kind of encouragement better than Paul, the writer of this letter to the church at Galatia.

Paul starts his first letter to the Corinthians (1:4) by telling them how he thanked God for them, and finishes his second letter to them by praying that they would "be made complete" in Christ (13:9).

- To the Galatians he prays a blessing over them (1:3).
- To the Philippians he declares: "I have you in my heart" (1:7).
- To the Colossians he says he is "praying always for you" (1:3).

What a thrill and encouragement it must have been for these believers, in far-off places, to hear that Paul was praying for them. In their many difficulties, persecution, and suffering… and also in their joys, they knew they were not alone. Someone was praying for them!

On one occasion when Archbishop Ben Kwashi arrived home to Jos, Nigeria, to discover that his wife was in hospital with multiple injuries after an assault by hostile Muslims, he cried out to God: "This should have been me! Why wasn't I here!"

God's response to his servant's broken heart was as clear as any spoken word: *Ben, the gates of Heaven have been bombarded by the prayers of saints from all over the world for you. When the praying people go to sleep in Europe, others are waking up in Australia; when they go to sleep in Australia, more are waking up in America, all of them pleading your case! And I have heard every prayer!*

And Archbishop Ben was overwhelmed by the outpouring of God's love, and the burden-bearing of others on his behalf.

If you are praying for someone – tell them!

If you need prayer – ask someone!

Remember Jesus' words to us: "By this all will know that you are My disciples, if you have love for one another" (John 13:35).

29

"... for I know whom I have believed and am persuaded that He is able to keep what I have committed to Him until that Day."

2 Timothy 1:12b

The sky was blue, yet again, on that final Sunday morning. Only a wisp of cloud dared to challenge my belief that God used just one colour to paint the sky above this place, so far from home.

However, the mood of our group contrasted with the glorious nature of the morning, each one of us subdued by all we had seen a mere twenty-four hours earlier in the refugee camps on the Thai/Burmese border.

My own silence was deepened by the fact that I was to speak at the church service in the Thai border town of Mae Sariang. What we had seen during the previous two weeks caused me to question the suitability of the talk I had prepared in the comfort of my study on the opposite side of the world. Added to which, I was to speak through an interpreter.

The service was as bright as the weather outside, in spite of the fact that the worship was led by orphans, and most of the congregation had lost everything. They had arrived in this ramshackle town with nothing – not even a country to call their own. I don't think I have ever felt more inadequate to deliver God's Word than when I stood up that day.

"God is able" were the first words to leave my mouth.

That was the theme of my talk. Yet the people listening had not experienced the rescue of parents, or the saving of their villages from evil men. But I continued, challenging my own heart as much as those who listened to believe the hard stuff – that God is able – in spite of the reality of heartache.

- God is able to save, I told them, because of the sacrifice His Son made for us.
- God is able to keep, not only our souls, when questions and disappointment threaten our faith, but…
- God is also able to keep what we have committed to Him – our families; our hopes; our dreams; our very lives.

By this stage the translator was nearly bouncing off the floor with excitement! And it hit me, as I watched her face thrill with that truth – that everyone they loved, and had left behind – God was able to keep!

And the truth stands wherever we reside, because we "know whom we have believed" – God can be trusted – "and [I] am persuaded that He is able to keep what I have committed to Him" (2 Timothy 1:12b).

But I wonder… have we committed *everything* to Him?

30

"This is real love – It is not that we loved God, but that he loved us and sent his Son as a sacrifice to take away our sins."

1 John 4:10 (NLT)

There are some things that we should never forget.

Or perhaps I should say that there are some things that we should decide to remember – like what the Son of God had to bear in His body on the tree... from me, and for me. It can be too easy to generalize Christ's atonement, recognizing that He died for the sins of the whole world, rather than to think of the state of our own hearts that pinned Him to that cross.

Lance Pibworth, co-founder of United Beach Mission, helps us to put it in perspective.

"All my sin of every kind; All the thoughts that stain my mind;
All the evil I designed... LAID ON HIM.
All the ways my feet have strayed; All the idols I have made;
All the times I have not prayed... LAID ON HIM.
All the told and acted lies; All success and all the tries;
Sins that I legitimise... LAID ON HIM.
All that sinks me to the mire; All the times of base desire;
All that needs a cleansing fire... LAID ON HIM.
All my misdirected powers; All my many wasted hours;

All my dreams of ivory towers… LAID ON HIM.
All that makes my spirit cold; All that keeps me from the fold;
All that dims my Father's gold… LAID ON HIM.
All the times I've grieved the Spirit; All the nature I inherit;
All the punishment I merit… LAID ON HIM.
LAID ON HIM, God's own dear Son; LAID ON HIM, the Holy One;
Blotting out the noonday sun… when LAID ON HIM."

Real love costs. Christ paid the price on the cross. Surely that is something we dare not forget?

31

"For by grace you have been saved through faith, and that not of yourselves; it is the gift of God, not of works, lest anyone should boast."

Ephesians 2:8–9

One of the most delightful gifts I received during this past year was when I visited my brother in Germany the week before Christmas.

The gift was an introduction to a beautiful little girl – a bittersweet gift, but one I was glad to receive. She reminded me so much of our own two daughters that at times I found it hard to keep back the tears.

Holding her in my arms was like pushing back time. Because of her disability, she couldn't support any of her own body weight… but I loved the closeness of her little form as I wrapped my arms around her, and relished the smell of her lovely brown hair. Her little feet twisted inwards at the end of stiff legs, while her fingers curled involuntarily around mine.

I found it heartbreaking to know that those feet once followed her big sister around the room, and those same fingers once played with favourite toys. Sadly they do so no longer, because this beautiful child has a dreadful degenerative condition that is stealing her away from her lovely family with alarming speed.

As she lay in my arms, it was easy to remember how our own girls, Cheryl and Joy, snuggled there for all those years that I had them in my life. And as I spoke with the little girl's mother I recognized the

same hopes and fears, joys and sorrows that had once been my experience.

However, it wasn't the sadness of her story, or the delight of holding her in my arms, that was the gift I wanted to share with you. It was the picture of her smile that made my heart leap and brought the thrill of joy that gave me such pleasure that Christmas. You see, if you have a child who can do nothing by herself, then a smile is not only their greatest achievement, but their best gift to you. It is far more precious than the most beautifully wrapped gift under any Christmas tree.

Today we tend to judge a gift by its price, or by the effort required in obtaining it. But surely the best gifts are those given from the heart.

And the very best gift of all was the one given from the heart of God. You know the one I mean, when "the Father sent his Son to be the Saviour of the world" (1 John 4:14 NLT). It's a gift that can't be bought or earned – but simply accepted – and enjoyed. A gift that, once received, will never be forgotten.

Thank you, my little German friend, for reminding me about it.

32

"And you will hear a voice say, 'This is the way; turn around and walk here.'"

Isaiah 30:21 (NLT)

DIVERSION

I dislike seeing that word stare at me from a bright yellow sign at the side of the road, especially when I'm in a hurry to get somewhere. But it's the big black arrow pointing out the alternative route that invariably makes me nervous. For you can be sure of one thing – it won't be a major road it will take you down.

Yet, occasionally, we see or experience something special because we have been forced to make a journey we hadn't planned. God is especially good at erecting DIVERSION signs, often at a time when we think we know exactly where we should be going, but He decides otherwise.

Take Joseph for example. He had neither planned to go to prison, nor did he deserve to be there. But God had Joseph take that diversion in his life so that he would meet the butler, who would in turn introduce him to Pharaoh. It was the long way round to the position God had planned for him, but it was essential to fulfil God's plan for Joseph, for Egypt, and more importantly for the preservation of the children of Israel (see Genesis 41).

God still works that way today.

One Monday morning I was forced to go into a shop to buy a replacement card for one that I'd lost. I was convinced I didn't have the time, but unknown to me, God had planned for me to share the Gospel message with the shop assistant on that very day. God diverted me to accomplish His purposes.

Yet sometimes my plans are so written in stone that there is barely room for the Holy Spirit to move them around. Oh, how we need to be willing to be diverted.

Are you praying for someone, or some situation, that you think cannot be changed? Trust God. For one day He is going to put a big yellow sign in front of another Christian, and divert them to the very person, or place, you need answers for.

So, the next time you are forced to head off in a direction you had no intention of taking, don't fight it. Instead, be ready for the person, or situation, God has planned for you to meet.

33

"Do not lay up for yourselves treasures on earth, where moth and rust destroy and where thieves break in and steal; but lay up for yourselves treasures in heaven, where neither moth nor rust destroys and where thieves do not break in and steal."

Matthew 6:19–20

The day the white charity van came was particularly difficult.

It had been only one week since my father-in-law's funeral. We had his clothes sorted, and the contents of his little flat packed into boxes, or unceremoniously left at the local amenity site. The speed of clearance seemed insensitive but was dictated by the letting contract he had previously signed.

"Contents" makes it sound a bit easier – not so personal – but then the van arrived and the boxes were loaded. All the little things that made Sammy who he was began to fill the van's gaping void – the books he would have spent ages telling you about, especially the ones about old Belfast; the mugs he liked to drink from, because so-and-so had brought it as a gift; his favourite reclining chair, where he stretched out after returning from playing the piano who-knows-where; the table where every night for the previous two and a half years he sat with Annie's photo in front of him, telling her how he had managed to fill another day without her. Sammy's bed was the last to

go, and we each grabbed a piece of it and headed outside.

Then, when the doors of the van slammed shut, the hole inside our hearts just got bigger, especially when my husband sighed the saddest of sighs. One man's life loaded into a white van, and that man his father – precious to all of us who knew him. It seemed indecent.

Returning to the empty flat I noticed a dusty white booklet lying on the floor where the bed had been. It had probably lain there for ages unnoticed, and I blew the dust from it as Philip followed me into the room. My heart leaped as I read out loud the words of the title written in large capitals: "**AT HOME WITH THE LORD.**"

In the midst of our tears, we had to smile. We'd been left a very precious reminder. A note from Heaven.

Sammy's things were only "things" after all. The bold-printed words reminded us that he had gone on to the place where he had already laid up his eternal treasure. The flat may have been empty, but the occupier had left a forwarding address.

34

"Be kind to each other, tenderhearted, forgiving one another, just as God through Christ has forgiven you."

Ephesians 4:32 (NLT)

It's likely that wherever you happen to be reading this, your government has a health strategy. In the UK it is called "The Health of our Nation".

Updated annually, this document sets out government health targets to decrease obesity and tobacco consumption, and to increase regular exercise and healthy eating habits. They want us to be fit for life.

Health is a single word which contains very broad terms of reference, including physical health; women's/men's health; sexual health; mental health; and developmental health. However, our government has omitted from all their documents something which impacts on our daily wellbeing, that of our spiritual health.

It is that part of us that has to do with our God-consciousness – undoubtedly neglected in its entirety by many, and needing frequent remedial attention by us all... not least in the area of forgiveness.

On one occasion I had the privilege of enjoying a meal with a forensic psychiatrist, who was also an advisor to the government on some of the most heinous crimes imaginable. I asked him a pretty predictable question about what makes people do these awful things, and become regarded as monsters in society.

He explained that though each case was complicated, most of the perpetrators could neither forgive what had previously been done to them, nor seek forgiveness for their own hearts.

Then, to my surprise, the eminent doctor went on to say that an unforgiving spirit, or an unforgiven life, wrecks not only the lives of the most hardened criminals, and their victims, but also the life of the ordinary man in the street. Forgiveness is vital, he added, not only for spiritual health, but also for emotional and physical health.

Vengeance and justice can seem so right in the light of wrongs committed against us, but the Bible tells us that we are to live differently. In fact we are to forgive "as God through Christ has forgiven you" (Ephesians 4:32 NLT).

It is not easy, but as a poster in our church hall says: "When we forgive, we set a prisoner free, and then we discover we were the prisoner."

It makes sense to choose freedom, by choosing forgiveness!

35

"Now godliness with contentment is great gain. For we brought nothing into this world, and it is certain we can carry nothing out."

1 Timothy 6:6–7

The ladies' weekend conference had been delightful.

At the final meal, I returned to the table carrying a delicious dessert only to discover the other delegates deep in discussion over the authenticity of the cheesecake. One lady was adamant that the said pie couldn't possibly be "the real thing", demonstrating reasons for her assumption as she picked through the layers with her fork.

The lovely fellowship we had been enjoying up to this point was seriously under threat, and all because seeds of discontent were being sown over a mere triviality.

There's always one, isn't there?

Someone in every group who loves to question, complain, or simply challenge what is going on around them. Too often it can be for the most trivial reasons. From the weather to the accommodation to how long the preacher speaks, the only predictable thing about this person is that they will complain.

Unfortunately it is all too easy to be that "one" ourselves, and to choose disgruntlement over contentment as our companion.

In Philippians 4:11 Paul had something much more serious on his mind – he was in prison. Yet we hear him say: "for I have learned in whatever state I am, to be content." Content, when his freedom had been removed? Yes! Content, even when he was facing execution? Yes!

How did Paul manage that? It obviously didn't come naturally, for he tells us that he had to learn it!

In a world that constantly encourages us to satisfy our own desires first, and to follow our own plans as a priority, Paul advises the opposite.

True reward, he explains, is found when we seek the kind of godliness that produces contentment (1 Timothy 6:6–7).

And contentment delivers peace.

36

"Now My eyes will be open and My ears attentive to prayer made in this place. For now I have chosen and sanctified this house, that My name may be there forever; and My eyes and My heart will be there perpetually."

2 Chronicles 7:15–16

The Temple had been finished and dedicated to the Lord. The praise party was over, and the people had gone home. Then in the stillness, the Lord Jehovah appeared to Solomon and made him the promise we have just read.

It would be in that very house, built for sacrifice and worship, that God promised He would watch over His people and hear their prayers – forever.

But Solomon's Temple is no more. The bricks and mortar are gone, and because of Christ's final atoning sacrifice, a new covenant has replaced the old. Yet a promise that was supposed to last "forever" had been made. Can it still be fulfilled?

Paul settles the question by his words in 1 Corinthians 6:19, and at the same time reminds us that God's promises always remain, even if circumstances change. "Do you not know," he says, "that your body is the temple of the Holy Spirit who is in you…?"

God no longer resides in temples built by hands, but in the lives of His children by the presence of His living Holy Spirit. We are His sanctified house today – His temple – each one of us created for worship and living sacrifice.

When the people left the dedication ceremony of Solomon's Temple they left "joyful and glad of heart" (2 Chronicles 7:10) having already offered praise by declaring: "For He is good, For His mercy endures forever" (2 Chronicles 7:3).

Even today we can discover that praise doesn't only bring delight to the heart of God, it can deliver joy to our hearts as well.

I can't help but wonder what God is hearing from each of His "temples" at this very moment?

37

"But by the grace of God I am what I am, and His grace toward me was not in vain."

1 Corinthians 15:10a

Occasionally I browse in a supermarket aisle that I rarely frequent anymore.

Every now and then it magnetizes me with its row upon row of dolls. Many years ago I used to walk those aisles with deep longings in my heart, wishing that I could buy one for Cheryl. For some reason these dolls – in flowing dresses or sporty jeans, accessorized with flashy cars or riding stables – seemed to epitomize what every girl would want, but all the while magnified what our own little girl could never enjoy.

Having been born profoundly disabled, Cheryl wasn't like other little girls. But the truth is she was different in ways other than what she couldn't do. I never could have imagined, when she was first placed in my arms, that I held a child who would be so mightily used by God, both in my own life, and in the lives of many others.

It was Cheryl who made me a mother; she who taught me to love expecting nothing in return; who drove me to the Scriptures; who made it possible for me to discover that God is a promise-keeping God – a God of great mercy, gentle patience, and abounding in love. She it was, who first caused me to mount a platform to speak of God's sustaining grace; who gave me the subject matter for my writing; who taught her younger brother to love unselfishly; who smiled when her baby sister Joy was placed in her arms for the first time. She it was, who stole the heart of her daddy when he first looked into her newborn face.

Yet in spite of the many tears shed over difficulties we wished she never had to experience, Cheryl brought a richness of joy into our lives which is difficult to put into words.

Of course we miss her, but Philip and I thank God for every one of the ten short years she beautified our lives. It is often through pain that we find the grace to do more than merely survive, but also to be moulded into the kind of people God wants us to be.

38

"My prayer is not for the world, but for those you have given me, because they belong to you."

John 17:9 (NLT)

"I've been praying for you."

I find it both humbling and encouraging when someone says these words to me. For almost twenty years people near and far prayed for us, and especially for our daughters, during many difficult days. More recently it's been my writing and speaking ministry that has motivated others to pray for me. Something brought into sharp focus when I was involved in a road traffic accident as I travelled home one night after a speaking engagement.

Neither my friend nor I was badly injured – "a miracle," the ambulance driver commented. "An answer to prayer," I responded as he and his colleague lifted me into the ambulance.

Wonderful and all as it is to know that other mortals are praying for us, and it is, there is something that amazes me even more.

Jesus has prayed for us, and He continues to do so!

In what has become known as Jesus' High Priestly Prayer, recorded for us in John 17, we are able to listen in as the saviour prays for His disciples before He leaves them, and then as He prays for us: "I am not only praying for these disciples," Jesus says to His Father, "but also for all who will ever believe in Me because of their testimony" (John 17:20 NLT).

Imagine – Jesus prayed for us! And this is what He prayed.

"Holy Father, keep them and care for them" (17:11 NLT).

"… keep them safe from the evil one" (17:15 NLT).

"My prayer for all of them is that they will be one" (17:21 NLT).

And don't you just love this next one?

"Father, I want these whom you've given Me to be with Me, so that they can see My glory" (17:24 NLT).

And on this very day Jesus continues to pray for us – He it is "who is even at the right hand of God, who also makes intercession for us" (Romans 8:34).

Be encouraged, you are on His heart – and one day you will share in His glory!

39

"And it came to pass after many days that the word of the LORD came to Elijah, in the third year, saying, 'Go, present yourself to Ahab, and I will send rain on the earth.'"

1 Kings 18:1

I wonder what Elijah thought when he heard those words?

Ahab, who "did more to provoke the LORD God of Israel to anger than all the kings of Israel who were before him" (1 Kings 16:33), was no friend of Elijah's. In fact they were mortal enemies. Ahab was after Elijah's blood! The evil, Baal-worshipping king had unsuccessfully scoured the country in an attempt to capture God's prophet.

Elijah had declared that God's judgement would come in the form of drought. And it hadn't rained in three years!

Meanwhile, Elijah was safely hiding in Zarephath, where God had told him to go. There, Elijah experienced the miraculous from God's hand, as did the poor widow who gave him shelter. He had food in time of drought; a roof over his head when he couldn't go home; and felt safe from the man who wanted him dead.

Why would he risk everything, including his life, and go back to Ahab?

Perhaps it was because Elijah had already proved that God could be trusted: with deliverance… with direction… with provision… with answered prayer. Perhaps it was also because Elijah already knew that God always kept His promises.

"Go, present yourself to Ahab," Elijah, God had said, "and I will send rain on the earth" (1 Kings 18:1).

Rain. A parched earth and a starving people needed rain. God had promised. Elijah believed. The prophet knew it was time to leave the place where he felt secure, and face his enemy once more. But Elijah recognized that he wouldn't be going to Ahab alone, and he was convinced that God would deliver both His servant, and His promise.

Leaving Zarephath wasn't so difficult after all!

Surely the safest place to be is in the centre of God's will? But we won't experience that sense of security for ourselves until we're brave enough to obey.

40

"Now may the God of hope fill you with all joy and peace in believing, that you may abound in hope by the power of the Holy Spirit."

Romans 15:13

Paul's farewells are legendary.

It seems that whether his letter had been instructive, corrective, or simply a message of greeting and encouragement, he always finished with words of cheer. Paul had a teacher's mind but a pastor's heart. He was well acquainted with the difficulties that many believers faced, especially those caused by persecution and personal heartache.

That's why the theology of hope was so important in Paul's communications. He wanted to leave them with something to look forward to, as well as a present confidence in God that would instil joy and peace in circumstances that in human terms seemed hopeless.

101

However, the hope that Paul wrote about was not a wishful thinking, pie-in-the-sky desire, perhaps in the way that we might hope for sunshine on our holidays. In fact it is quite the opposite.

To "hope" in biblical terms is to be certain of something that has not yet been realized. Hope is the promise still to be fulfilled, with the assurance that it will be. Hope is an absolute, not a maybe.

The God of hope that Paul speaks about in this verse is the God whose promises have been secured for us through His Son. That's how we can know "joy and peace" even when life is tough. And our certainty – hope – for what lies ahead comes through believing what has already been confirmed in Christ.

"And this hope will not lead to disappointment. For we know how dearly God loves us, because he has given us the Holy Spirit to fill our hearts with his love" (Romans 5:5 NLT).

This "hope" has the power to push back any form of darkness we might find ourselves in!

Special thanks

No project can be completed without the help of others. On this occasion a special word of thanks goes to Tony Collins, Jenny Ward, and the excellent team at Monarch for your encouragement, advice, and expertise. It's a pleasure to work with you.

Before my writing reaches the Monarch team, it has already been sifted and shaken by my husband Philip, and good friend, Liz Young. Thanks guys. Maybe one day you won't have to use as much red ink!

Catherine would love to hear from you, and you can make contact via:

www.catherine-campbell.com
www.facebook.com/catherinecampbellauthor
www.catherine-campbell.com/blog

Picture Acknowledgments

Alan Bedding: p. 100–101

Andrew King: pp. 10–11, 12, 40–41, 44–45, 51, 66–67, 103

Estelle Lobban: pp. 8–9, 19, 21, 30, 32, 48–49, 62, 76–77, 86, 90, 92, 94

Getty: p. 54 Joshua McCullough

iStock: pp. 24 Ukapala; 25 Jenjen42; 28 Motimeiri; 39 Technotr;
47 Anna Bryukhanova; 58 Chepko; 88 Dem10

Jean Picton: pp. 4, 9, 26, 33, 42, 52, 55, 58, 63, 69, 74, 80, 84, 94, 102, 109

Len Kerswill: pp. 16, 23, 37, 56, 60, 68, 81

Mission Aviation Fellowship: p. 71 Mark and Kelly Hewes

Roger Chouler: pp. 5, 7, 34–35, 43, 65, 73, 75, 78–79, 82, 84, 96–97, 99, 105

Shutterstock: p. 14 Vitality Mateha

Other books by Catherine Campbell:

ISBN: 978-1-85424-983-8

ISBN: 978-0-85721-223-8

ISBN: 978-0-85721-612-0

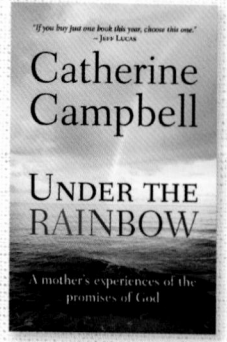

ISBN: 978-0-85721-445-4

ISBN: 978-0-85721-289-4